Dedicat:

I dedicate these memoir Franky, who deciphered my scr spelling and grammar - and ur ⌐ ⌐ expand upon some of the stories that she said I had cut short.

Also to my daughter Carolyn, who pointed out the parts of the story that might not be understood by her generation - and to my daughter Angie, who urged me to do it in the first place.

But perhaps the biggest dedication should go to my very good friend Bert, who was the real Desert Rat.

The War Memoirs of Adrian Jucker

For some time now, the family has been asking me to write down some of my wartime experiences, and as I am now seventy-six and my memory is already getting very shaky, I had better get down to it before it is too late.

I am not going to write a saga of great adventures, or attempt to give any kind of history of the war. There are plenty of other, far better sources of this information than I could possibly provide. Instead, I will try to give a few glimpses of what it was like to live through those frightening, tedious, uncomfortable, sometimes exciting and often tragic times.

I shall begin at the beginning…

Chapter I

One fine September morning in 1939, my mother and I - and I think my sister Angela, were listening to the radio when the words of Neville Chamberlain came through, to tell us that we were now at war with Germany. The news did not come as any surprise. In some ways it was a relief to know that at last we were going to do something to challenge the dreadful Nazi regime that we saw as the most evil thing the world had ever known.

At that time, we had already heard of the Nazi treatment of the Jews and of their Concentration Camps. The German people had also heard about it but refused to believe, or at least pretended not to believe that it was happening. Hitler's ideas of creating a 'Greater Germany' by invasion had already become self-evident.

That same day I went down to the recruiting office in Haslemere and signed on as a gunner in the Royal Artillery. I received a day's pay. Not quite 'the King's shilling' but, if I remember, about two shillings and sixpence. I chose the Artillery because my brother Philip had been in the artillery Territorials, and I always tried to do whatever Philip had done. I expected to be called up in a few days' time to go and do my bit across the Channel. I was, in those days, quite ignorant of the inscrutable workings of the military mind. From the day I was enrolled in the Royal Artillery in September 1939 to the present time I never heard another word from them. Perhaps in some obscure long forgotten file in the War Office you will find 'Gunner Jucker, missing, presumed deserter'.

The early months of the war were spent in Haslemere, fixing blackout screens on all the windows and putting adhesive tape across the glass. We also arranged an air raid shelter in the wine cellar and put in some form of heating. One of the results of this was that at the end of the war we inherited a large stock of rather expensive vinegar.

Our life in Haslemere was considerably enlivened when we took in four or five evacuee children from the East End of London. They were a really charming bunch, very bright and extremely noisy.

When they asked "What should we call you, Mister?" I said "Call me Uncle Adrian", and after that we got on very well indeed. The brightest and youngest was Bernie. One day Bernie asked "Is Auntie June your tart?" and as I understood the language, I told him that she was. And of course she still is.

After the summer 'vac' of 1940 I went back to Cambridge expecting to be called up any day, but as months went by and final exams got nearer, I began to worry. Studying for my finals had **not** been top of my agenda for some time. When news came round that the army wanted to recruit a ski unit to go to Finland I jumped at the chance. For some reason they wanted to form a Survey unit that could ski, and as my maths was reasonably good and I could ski, I thought I had a chance of being accepted. The War Office called me to an interview in London and I went, hoping to convince them that I had a working knowledge of spherical trigonometry, which I had, and that I was an expert skier, which I was not. I was still ignorant of the workings of the military mind and was surprised that what the interviewers were trying to find out was whether or not I was socially acceptable as 'officer material'. Apparently I did pass the test, and, as I was by now beginning to understand the way things happen in the army, I was not unduly surprised to find that, having volunteered to join a ski unit, I should be posted to North Africa.

My daughter has pointed out to me that the words 'socially acceptable' and 'officer material' would not only be considered politically incorrect but are almost impossible to understand in today's world, so I will try to explain what those words meant in 1939.

In the pre-war services, it was presumed without question that an officer was a 'Gentleman'. This did not mean that every 'Gentleman' would qualify to be an officer, but on the other hand it would be difficult for someone who did not appear to be a 'Gentleman' to be considered as 'Officer Material', particularly in the smarter Infantry regiments and, for example, in the Eleventh Hussars. The R.A.F, The Tank Corps and the Royal Engineers were more democratic in this respect, but the Royal Navy was not. This attitude of the military selection boards was not quite as silly as it sounds today. Boys like myself, who had been to Public School, would nearly all have spent five years in the School Officer Training Corps, learning the basic skills to become an officer. For example, I had, since the age of twelve, been learning to drill with, and to fire, the Lee Enfield rifle that had been used in the 1914-18 war. By the age of thirteen, I had qualified as a 'First Class Shot', as had many of my contemporaries.

To qualify for a commission in the smarter Cavalry regiments one had to show a decent standard of horsemanship. Since most farms had become mechanised, the only boys who could ride a horse had fathers who could afford to send them to riding school. The fact that horsemanship was a one time prerequisite of a commission in the Eleventh Hussars, the 'Cherry Pickers', who set so much of the tone of the Seventh Armoured Division, might today seem odd, since that regiment went to war in armoured cars. As I have said already, the Military mind worked on a different wavelength from that of civilians, but it must be said that the system seemed to work.

However, before that happened we have the moment when nothing stood between this green and pleasant land and the might of the Third Reich, but Sapper Jucker and five rounds of ammunition, helped by a few friends.

The story of the battle of Portsdown Ridge will not be found in any of the history books, so I will tell it now, before it is forgotten forever. Like so many dramatic moments in my life it caught me with my pants down, literally. I was on the loo in Fort Widley - one of the large fortresses at Portsdown built to keep out Napoleon - when the alarm sounded to tell us that the German invasion had started.

Although Fort Widley was a fortress of most impressive impregnability, some military genius had decided that we should abandon the fort and defend England from small slit-trenches dug into the limestone of Portsdown Ridge, from which position we would drive off the German Panzer divisions with rifle and bayonet.

Someone had overlooked the fact that as the ridge curved gently in a downward slope, the approaching enemy would be completely hidden from sight until about fifty yards away. I forgot to mention that we were also armed with a most ingenious hand grenade, made from empty food cans containing a stick of gelignite, a detonator, a ten second fuse and a handful of assorted scrap iron. The only effective way of lighting the fuse on a windy night was with a lighted cigarette. Thus, armed to the teeth, we waited all night.

The night passed without excitement for me, but one of my brave comrades had his moment of glory. In the small hours of the morning a head appeared advancing over the curving ridge.

"Halt, who goes there?" he called. There was no answer, so he called again as required by our orders. Still no answer, so he fired one of his precious five rounds of ammunition, and the head dropped from sight. In the morning, after the all-clear was sounded, he discovered that he had shot a cow clean through the forehead.

That cow was the only casualty of the Battle of Portsdown Ridge. We never found out why the alarm was sounded, because the invasion never happened, that night or any other.

Many years later I spoke to a gunner officer who was also at Fort Widley and he tells me that the artillery had only five rounds of ammunition per gun. It seems that at that time the defenders of this sceptered isle were no better equipped than Dad's Army. Thank God for the Royal Air Force and the Royal Navy!

I had embarkation leave, and June and I decided to have a night out in London. That was the night we could not get a table at the Café de Paris. In spite of the heavy air raids, London was packed with people in pubs and restaurants. By today's standards everything was absurdly cheap. Dinner at the Café Royal cost five shillings, and a bottle of Algerian Red (almost the only wine available) was about two and six a bottle, or less. We had dinner at Gennaro's in Soho, and every time a bomb dropped, we looked at the mirrors all round the restaurant.

That night, we had a room on the fifth floor of the Regents Palace Hotel, which had a reputation for naughty goings on. We didn't get much sleep that night because air raids went on most of the night. In the morning, we learned that the Café de Paris, where we had **tried** to get a table, had been bombed, killing everyone on the dance floor, including 'Snake-Hips Johnson' and his famous band. Nine months later Franky was born.

Chapter II

After embarkation leave and a short stay in Halifax, I was sent to join a troop ship in Liverpool harbour. My troop ship was a luxury P&O liner, and I was given a comfortable cabin and told that dinner would be at seven. When the dinner bell sounded, my fellow officers and I went to the dining room and were shown to a table by a waiter. When we saw the menu, we thought it must be a joke. At that time food rationing was very strict and, in fact, one could not always get the ration expected. But here in Liverpool harbour the 'P&O' offered the full, peace-time, five course dinner menu. It was not a joke. We ate the full P&O menu for two months on that ship. Being P&O, one of the luxury liners which used to carry passengers to India, one of the specialities was, of course, curry. They gave us a different curry every night and only started repeating themselves when we got to the Red Sea.

We moved out of harbour on March 11th 1941, which was also my 21st birthday. I didn't know when, or even whether, I would see my wife, June again – and although it was too early to know that she was pregnant, it was certainly a possibility. In a moment of nostalgia for everything I was leaving behind, I wrote a letter to my unborn son, whom I might never meet. It was to be opened on the occasion of *his* 21st birthday. I later posted the letter, but it has since vanished, which may be just as well, since the baby was, in fact, a girl.

As we moved out of harbour, we formed up into one of the biggest convoys ever sent out: a long convoy of troop ships drawn up in two line-ahead columns, surrounded by destroyers and corvettes and minesweepers. The escort kept racing round the slow moving troop ships like sheep-dogs with a flock of sheep. We were, in fact, attacked several times by German U-boats, but we didn't lose a single ship.

Many years later, I found myself having dinner with a German who told me he was a U-boat commander who tried to break through our escort. We compared dates and it was certainly our convoy which he tried to attack off the west coast of Africa. We had sailed within sight of the neutral Azores and that is probably how the U-boats got our location.

Our pleasure cruise took us on a zigzag course right across the Atlantic to within sight of Bermuda, then south and east to Freetown in West Africa, then on to Cape Town. I shall never forget the beautiful harbour with Table Mountain as a backcloth. When we anchored for the night, we dragged ourselves away from the dining room, duty-free drinks in hand, to see the harbour all lit up. It was the first time since the war started that we had seen a town without any blackout.

We had three days shore leave at Cape Town. When we went ashore, we found a convoy of cars waiting to take us to bars, restaurants and even to people's homes. The hospitality shown us was quite unforgettable. And, of course, food rationing was unheard of in South Africa.

One last memory of Cape Town: as we sailed out of harbour, a young lady stood at the end of the quay and sang to us. She had a lovely voice and, presumably, some amplifier, because we could hear her voice until we were right out at sea. I have heard since then that she sang out every convoy and became quite famous, I don't know her name and I am afraid I can't remember what she sang, but the memory is still with me.

You might expect that when we eventually landed in Egypt my life of luxury would come to an end, but in fact I was to spend several months in Cairo and then in Alexandria, living in comparative comfort. The food was excellent, and I mean army food as well as the food in restaurants.

All drink was cheap and at that time there were no shortages of anything. The war was literally miles away in the desert. We sapper officers were not quite as spoilt as the officers at GHQ in Cairo, who wore smart tailor-made gabardine uniforms and would be found round the bar at Shepheards Hotel or Groppi's restaurant. We used to refer to them rather scathingly as either the Gabardine Swine or Groppi's Light Horse.

I have never despised anyone for making himself as comfortable as possible under the circumstances, though I have occasionally been just a little jealous. It seems to me that any damn fool can make himself uncomfortable if he chooses to do so. Even in Normandy, I managed to have two eggs for breakfast and my shirts washed and pressed and scented with lavender: the trick was to pick out the best scrounger in the unit and make him my batman, and threaten him with a real job of work if he ever let me down.

All good things come to an end, and so one day I found myself in the desert. The desert is not what you expect - blazing sun and endless sand dunes. In fact the so-called Western Desert is mostly hard rock with a thin coating of dust, and although it can be very hot in summer, the winter nights were often bitterly cold. Not quite freezing, but with a cold wind that seemed to blow right through you.

The dust was as fine as face powder and penetrated everywhere, but the real plague of the desert was the flies. Not mosquitoes, but ordinary (or extraordinary) flies. The quantity and persistence of the flies was almost unbelievable. The flies were desperately short of water, so they made for your lips and your eyes. Fortunately flies cannot see in the dark, so we got some peace at night. Because of their dirty feeding habits the flies infected any food they could touch and any cut on your skin. Even a spot could become a running ulcer - desert sores we called them, and we nearly all got them sooner or later. Apart from the flies and the dust and the cold night wind in the winter, the food and drink situation was not quite up to P&O standards. Bully beef is quite good when served from the fridge with a little fresh salad on a summer's day in England. But served warmish so that you pour it out of the tin, and accompanied by a dry army biscuit, it gets a bit depressing when it is your staple diet for several months on end.

Water was always scarce, sometimes more so than at other times. In good times we sometimes had a gallon a day, but quite often it was down to half a gallon. That was for all purposes, including washing.

In the heat of summer, one needed to drink four pints a day. That's half a gallon, so washing did not get a high priority. The Army still insisted we should shave every day, so we used the last dregs of our morning mug of tea for this purpose. I developed the two shirt system: you wore one shirt until you couldn't stand the smell of it, then you changed to the second shirt and wore it until it was even worse. By this time the first shirt seemed comparatively acceptable, so you changed again. You could keep this up for several months, and sometimes you did.

Now that we are on the subject of food and drink (surprise, surprise!) let me explain the very simple and effective way the Eighth Army made its essential mug of tea. In the days before the British Army made a rather inferior copy of the German petrol can, called the Jerry can, our petrol came in two gallon square tin containers. With a tin opener, one cut the empty petrol can in half, one half was then partly filled with sand, and a measure of petrol was poured onto the sand and set alight, the other half can was then filled with water and placed on top of the first half can, and a suitable amount of tea was thrown into the cold water. No nonsense of boiling the water first, the tea was stewed to form a really strong brew which the British soldier preferred.

Connoisseurs would float a dead match on top of the water. This was believed to take away the taste of petrol, which was always a feature of the desert tea.

Occasionally we came across a wandering Arab. Senousi Bedouins always dressed in black, and the more dashing ones would be riding a German BMW motorbike, left behind by the German Army. A bargaining session would then begin to exchange tea for eggs. Both sides were experts at this, and would start off by offering brewed tea leaves dried in the sun in exchange for addled eggs. These preliminaries concluded, with no hard feelings on either side, real tea would be exchanged for moderately fresh eggs. Unlike the Egyptian Arabs who are great coffee drinkers, the Senousi of Libya prefer tea, which they sometimes drink with mint.

As we never had any fresh meat in the desert, I managed to shoot a few gazelles. The liver was particularly delicious, and the haunch was also very good. We roasted this in a metal ammunition box, which made an excellent oven. I always used a discarded Italian rifle and ammunition for hunting, as we were not supposed to use our own.

One of my first jobs in the desert was when I was working for a survey company. As much of the desert is completely flat and featureless, there is nothing much to put on a map. I once heard an argument between two sappers as to whether there was more fuck all on one side than there was bugger all on the other side. I cannot put it better than that. To overcome this problem, I had the job of constructing beacons, consisting of two empty 40 gallon oil drums one on top of the other. We would mount these on a small pile of stones and mix a bucketful of concrete to put on the bottom, with a number scratched into it. These beacons would be in sight of one another, so that anyone reading the number would know where he was on the map.

We covered hundreds of square miles of desert with these beacons, often far behind what could be described as the front line. We would drive off into the blue with two Bedford 15 cwt trucks and a three ton truck for the oil drums, water and petrol. We never ran into any German or Italian patrols. In this we were luckier than one man we picked up, at least a hundred miles from anywhere. He had been driving an ambulance when he was attacked by a German fighter plane. He was the only survivor - and was walking alone without any water and with two bullet wounds in his shoulder. As we were on our way to Bir Hakeim we took him there, and left him with a French doctor from the Foreign Legion. The man's name was Corporal Gill, and I often wonder what happened to him.

During these trips into the remoter areas of the Libyan desert we saw a lot of gazelle, and on one occasion I saw through my binoculars what looked rather like a donkey with very long horns. I think it must have been an oryx, but those animals are not supposed to be anywhere near that region, so I have no explanation. Another surprise was to see a very large grey shaggy dog, or wolf perhaps. It looked like an Irish wolf hound. Again, I have no explanation.

We saw plenty of desert rats hopping along like tiny kangaroos, and at one time, near Tobruk, we made a pet of one. At the time, I was sharing a dug-out with two other officers when the 'rat' appeared. I went to chase it out, but you can't chase something that doesn't move away. The rat simply sat there washing its face. This is something that psychiatrists call 'disassociated behaviour'. In other words, when faced with a situation that one doesn't understand one does something unrelated to the actual situation.

After this introduction, the desert rat became a very special pet. We offered him army biscuits which he very wisely refused, so we tried him with chocolate. This, he went for in a big way. Someone (probably me) very naughtily tried him on gin. We poured a little gin into the lid of a tobacco tin and the desert rat (his name was Bert, by the way, because he was as fat as our Quarter Master of that name) put his nose into the gin and jumped back about two feet and sat up washing his face. After a short time he came back to try again. This time he didn't jump back quite so far and, after due consideration, Bert decided that he rather liked gin and came back and really lapped it up. Weight for weight it would be like a man drinking a whole bottle.

This had a curious effect on Bert. He performed a kind of wall-of-death act, running round the completely vertical walls of the dug-out three or four times, an amazing acrobatic feat, defying all the laws of gravity - and common sense.

We became very fond of Bert - but when we had to move on he absolutely refused to be put in a box so that we could take him with us. I am ashamed to say that we left an alcoholic gerbil wandering round the desert looking for gin and chocolate.

Having joined the R.E. Survey in order to go skiing in Finland, the Survey Department and I found that we were not really suited to each other and I was posted to a real Engineer unit. The job of an engineer in the Army is to build bridges, blow up bridges, defuse unexploded bombs and to lay and clear minefields, and during the next few years I did some of all these things. But in the desert it was mines, mines and more mines. I became something of an expert on the subject.

There is talk nowadays of getting an international agreement against the use of mines, and I am completely in agreement with this idea. All over the world, mostly in the Third World, mines are laid by the million, in unmarked areas, where they inflict horrible injuries on innocent civilian populations, particularly children. In the Western Desert, minefields were laid between clearly marked wire fences. Neither the Eighth Army nor the Afrika Korps ever laid mines loosely scattered in areas where civilians could walk onto them. We laid anti-tank mines as a protective barrier against surprise tank attacks and we laid anti-personnel mines among them to slow down the enemy sappers, who would try to clear the mines, and as a defence against surprise infantry attack. We always made detailed maps of where each mine was laid, so that they could be removed easily and safely.

All this sounds reasonably ethical on the face of it. Unfortunately very few of the mines were removed at the end of the war, and as the Bedouins first 'stole' the wire for their own use, some minefields became unmarked and wandering camels, goats and Bedouins were injured or killed as a result. The Egyptian government was supposed to be given maps of all minefields laid on Egyptian soil, but I don't believe very much was done to make the area safe. A few years ago, the Egyptian government asked the British, Italian and German governments to send out 'experts' to help them clear the minefields. I wrote to the Chief Engineer telling him that I probably knew more about the mines laid by the British than any other Engineer Officer in the army. I offered to go without pay, but the offer was very politely refused. I didn't make this offer out of any very altruistic motive, I just thought it would be interesting to meet the German and Italian officers who had laid the minefields at El Alamein.

You may have noticed that so far in these notes I have not mentioned anything that could be described as fighting, and that is because, from the day I signed on as a gunner, nearly three years were to pass before I heard a shot fired in anger, except of course for air raids, which everyone in England had experienced many times.

Unlike the 1914-18 war, we didn't live in trenches within spitting distance of the enemy. In fact until the El Alamein confrontation there was no very clear 'front line' at all. The first time I ever actually saw the enemy in the flesh, so to speak, was in August 1942, during the battle of Alam Halfa. My troop had been laying minefields which were part of the trap into which Monty had lured the Afrika Korps. Monty deliberately left open what appeared to be a breakthrough to Cairo and the Suez Canal, which was the prize Rommel hoped to win. My job was to close the last gap in the minefield before the enemy arrived, and then draw back to our next prepared position.

It was a bit spooky knowing that all the British troops had withdrawn and that we were the last to leave. We had just completed re-laying mines to close the gap, when the whole night sky lit up with Very lights, so that it was almost as bright as day. Then we saw them, two or three thousand German soldiers marching in a long line stretched out in both directions and only just a few hundred yards away. There were German soldiers as far as the eye could see. There was something almost unreal about it, rather like watching an Aldershot Tattoo or some elaborate historical pageant. I can remember having no sense of danger, we just quietly withdrew, without, of course, firing a shot.

Chapter III

This part of my story must bring us to Alamein. Not everyone knows that there were two battles of Alamein, the first, we lost, the second, we won. I was in both of them.

The first battle of Alamein was fought under the command of General Auchinleck. It was intended to break through the German front and force the enemy back. You might think that as I was there I should be able to tell you what happened, but in fact I simply don't know. When you are in a battle you only know what is happening in your immediate field of vision and what is reported to you. This is how it happened.

I was in command of a troop of sappers detached from the rest of the company. We were given no specific task to perform and were told to wait in a certain area until given further orders. Early in the night we could hear the noise of gun fire, and so we knew that an attack had started. Still no orders came to do anything. We waited several hours and then a column of vehicles, tanks and Bren-carriers started moving past our position, in the direction away from the front. This went on for several more hours until eventually there were no more vehicles passing and there was almost complete silence.

The British Army never retreats, it 'withdraws to prepared positions', so it seemed sensible to me to follow everyone else. The dust thrown up by this column of vehicles made visibility limited to a few yards, so we just followed the vehicle in front crawling along at snail's pace, with frequent stops and starts. This went on until daylight, when presumably we had reached 'prepared positions', and the withdrawal was halted. Fortunately the enemy did not follow us. Perhaps he had problems of his own.

When I tried to find out what had happened I got the impression of complete confusion, what is vulgarly referred to as 'a bugger's muddle'.

Shortly after this, Monty took over command of the Eighth Army, and things started to change very rapidly.

To explain the general situation, what had been happening in the desert for the last two years was a sort of yo-yo action back and forth. First we beat the Italian army back as far as Benghazi, that is about six hundred miles west of El Alamein. Then the German Afrika Korps arrived and drove us back. This retreat was so fast that we used to refer to it as the Benghazi handicap. Then the Germans somehow lost the initiative and we drove them back again, but not for long, because, under Rommel, the Germans came back in force and we withdrew to 'prepared positions' behind the Alamein line. The Alamein line was a defensive barrier of minefields and it had been the job of my unit, 295 Field Squadron, R.E., to lay a very large share of this.

I have already mentioned that things changed when Montgomery arrived, and I will try to explain what happened. The Eighth Army had begun to get the impression that the only general who knew his arse from his elbow was Rommel, and I am not sure that we were wrong. Until Monty arrived Generals were something that one knew about but never actually saw. Monty changed this with a terrific P.R. exercise. He personally visited every unit in the Eighth Army and gave us one of his pep talks. These talks were always full of references to cricket. We were told that we were going to 'hit the enemy for six'. Somehow he sounded convincing and the morale improved enormously.

Monty's first move was the battle of Alam Halfa, which I have already written about. This was completely successful in that it lured the bulk of the German Afrika Korps to the south, where it hoped to break through to Cairo and

Alexandria while Monty was preparing for a major attack in the north, his great battle of El Alamein.

The preparation of the battle was like the preparation of a great stage event. We actually held two dress rehearsals in which we went through all the actions that we would have to do on the night. For the first time since I joined the army I knew exactly what I had to do and exactly how to do it. It was a very refreshing feeling.

With a troop of sappers, my job was to clear a gap through two minefields to allow the tanks through to attack and drive back the enemy and then to follow through and drive him out of Africa.

The day of the 23rd October was spent waiting for the start of the action, which was to be at twenty to ten. I explained to my troop exactly what we had to do and the enormous importance of our success. I remember thinking of Henry V's speech to his troop before Harfleur, and it then occurred to me that it was a load of codswallop. You simply don't talk to soldiers on the eve of battle about 'stiffening the sinews' and 'imitating the action of the tiger'. You tell them exactly what the odds are and what the plan is, and above all the importance of their particular part in that plan. I don't suppose it was a great speech, and it certainly would not have sounded half as good as Shakespeare's does on the stage. But we were not on the stage and most of us knew that we would probably be dead before the play was over.

One other thing: we were issued with a rum ration before the action, and believe it or not I did not issue the rum to my troop. I told my men that I was not taking a lot of drunks into a minefield and that we would drink it after the job was done.

At exactly 21.40 hours on the 23rd October 1942, the biggest bang of artillery the world had ever heard shook the earth. The battle had started, and one thousand guns all fired together.

We were one mile from the enemy front line: one mile of open desert across which we marched. We marched with the Highland Division and we were right in the front, next to the piper. The night sky was lit up by coloured tracer shells, and it really was a fantastic sight which I can never forget. The piper kept playing right up to the German minefield, which we reached at exactly ten o'clock.

A word now about how we were dressed and equipped for the big night. We were in light summer uniform, I wore trousers instead of shorts because shorts are very uncomfortable for crawling in. Over this I wore a leather jerkin, the nights were quite cold in October. I wore it inside out, because the leather would shine in the moonlight and being a shy sort of person I didn't want to draw attention to myself. For weapons, I had a Thompsons submachine gun, the famous Tommy gun of the old gangster movies. I also had a .38 revolver and a bayonet, not for fighting but for prodding the ground for mines. I also had a pair of pliers, a few one and a half inch nails and a small coin. The nails were used to make safe anti-personnel mines and the small coin fitted into a slot on the German 'Teller' anti-tank mine, to make it safe. The Teller mine also had two ingenious booby trap devices underneath, which you had to remove by hand before lifting them.

My job was first to cut the wire, then to go through the minefield followed by my sergeant, who had to lay out a white tape to mark the way that I had cleared. To cut the wire, which was about five strands if I remember, I had to lie on my back and cut it from underneath. This was fairly easy, and I started to crawl forward searching the ground with a bayonet to find the mines. I was not worried about anti-tank mines because my weight was not enough to set them off (no comments please), but I had to look out for anti-personnel mines, which were real killers.

I soon came to my first anti-personnel mine. This was an Italian mine fastened to a post with a trip wire, which I cut with a pair of pliers. I then needed to place a one and a half inch nail in a hole at the top of the mine. There was no hole! This was worrying, but the next step was to pull out the detonator, and the bloody detonator would not come out. My hands were sweating by this time and I nearly panicked. I took a few big breaths and began to think. Then I realised what had happened: the Italian sapper who had laid the mine had not set it properly. It was not fused or primed. It was quite harmless. After that I came across several Italian mines that had not been properly set up. Looking back on it I will never know whether the Italian sappers had not been properly trained or whether they were afraid of the mines (which were very dodgy) or even whether the Italians hadn't got their hearts into fighting alongside the Germans.

After the slight setback of this Italian mine, things got easier, until I came right up to the enemy wire at the other side of the minefield. This was a very formidable obstacle, about ten feet high and ten feet wide, made of concertina wire, and I could see the quite deadly German 'S' mines that were fastened inside it as booby traps.

I fastened a battery torch with a white light on this wire, facing, of course, away from the enemy. This was to show my men that I had reached the end of the minefield, and I and my sergeant then started back, following our white tape. While all this was happening a battle was raging all around us. The men of the Highland regiments were fighting their way forward and the enemy was firing back with everything he had, enemy tracer bullets were flying all round us, and these of course were only the ones we could see.

At this moment there was a loud bang and I was struck very hard on the back of the leg. I remember slapping my hand down very hard and being relieved to find that my leg was still there. I told my sergeant I had been hit and could not walk. He was a splendid man called Sergeant Ball, who had the whitest teeth I have ever seen. I remember those teeth grinning at me and telling me quite calmly that he had been hit too and could not help. For some reason we both laughed and said "Well, now we can go to hospital and be looked after by some lovely nurses".

Sergeant Ball and I were carried back by some of our men to the beginning of the minefield. We applied first aid dressings to our wounds to stop them bleeding. Sergeant Ball was in a worse state than I was, and I arranged for a stretcher party to carry him back.

The next thing I had to do was to send forward a Bangalore Torpedo. This was a very simple device consisting of a metal pipe full of explosive, which was to be pushed under the wire at the far end of the minefield and detonated. It was completely effective and made a wide gap in the wire. I believe this was the only time a Bangalore Torpedo had been used since 1918. After this I sent in the mine-sweeping party, which consisted of three men with mine detectors, followed by three men carrying little cardboard hats. These hats were placed wherever the mines were found. Three more men followed, whose job was to lift the mines and place them on the side of the cleared track. As a track was cleared, a white tape was laid to show the edge of the cleared space. If any man was killed or wounded his place was taken by the man behind him so that the clearing process did not stop.

At this stage a doctor arrived, put a more effective bandage on my wound and said he would carry me back on his jeep. I simply could not agree to this because there was no-one else I could leave to run the show. A few days before the battle I had been given a second sergeant, but he had not been present for all the training and did not know the mine clearing drill. He was also, as I could see, in a state of almost paralysing shock and quite useless. I sent him back 'to look after the stores' or something that he would be able to do.

I was lucky to have a really first class Corporal, who from then on took on the burden of doing my sergeant's job and some of mine as well. (I recommended him for the MM, which I believe he received). I am afraid I have forgotten his name.

To continue, as the clearing proceeded we stuck iron posts on either side of the cleared gap, these posts had an iron plate like a 'T' on top which was painted red and white, and we fixed a green light on the white side and a red light on the red side. This made a very pretty sight when it was finished: a track about thirty feet wide with red and green lights on each side.

We were expecting to have to clear a gap through two minefields. Then, when these were clear, we were to send back the code 'Mary Jane'. However we found a third minefield, so I sent back the code 'Mary Jane has had a baby'.

When our job was finished, our order was to dig slit trenches for ourselves just before the last minefield and wait there. Waiting was one of the things that occupied most of one's time in the army. Unfortunately we had been given a very bad place to wait. The enemy knew exactly where his minefields were, and by this time must have known where the gaps were, so, very sensibly, he aimed an artillery barrage on the last gap and continued shelling for the rest of the night and most of the morning. Unfortunately that was where we were lying.

The light Valentine tanks of the Armoured Brigade passed through our gaps before daylight, and then when it was full day (I can't remember the time) the Sherman tanks passed through. This was the first time we had seen Sherman Tanks. They had been sent from America just in time for El Alamein. I should mention that the first American tank, the Grant tank, was a total failure. It had a gun on a turret that could not be pivoted, so that you had to point the whole tank at the target. Worse still, it had a petrol engine! The poor men who had to go to war in a Grant tank called them 'Mobile Crematoriums'.

Sometime during the day, I had an order from the commander of the armoured brigade to go and blow up a tank which was stuck in a minefield, about two hundred yards in front of their forward position. It was thought that a German sniper was in the tank. I did not believe for one moment that there was a sniper or anyone else in the tank, but obeying stupid orders was something one became used to, and in any case it looked a fairly simple job.

By this stage of the battle my armoured car had caught up with us, and I always carried a fairly comprehensive supply of explosives in it. Although the tank was evidently in a minefield, it was possible to see mines fairly easily in daylight: the wind would blow the sand covering the mines into a tell-tale little mound, or even expose the mine completely.

My plan was to drive up to the tank, drop a large charge of explosive through the open hatch and then drive back.

Unfortunately I had not been as clever as I thought, and we hit a mine. The armoured car jumped up like a bucking horse and then settled down with a thump. The engine stopped and we were on fire. I had a driver and my batman with me and I told them to run for it before we blew up. (My batman, by the way, was an interesting fellow, a poacher by trade and the only man I ever met who called a partridge a perdrix. For some reason he never wore socks under his boots and although almost illiterate, he had an uncanny sense of direction and was an inveterate scrounger.)

I watched these two run like hell in a zigzag way because some unkind German (or Italian) was shooting at them with a machine gun. I think they broke the Olympic record for two hundred metres.

At this point my own situation didn't look too promising: the armoured car was starting to burn quite nicely, and it was a toss-up whether the fire reached the petrol or my explosives and detonators first. I certainly could not run and didn't fancy crawling with a machine gunner using me for target practice. I was also very, very tired and had reached the point where I didn't care very much one way or another. I can remember thinking of June receiving a telegram saying I had been killed, and I just could not bear the thought. At this point someone in the armoured brigade had the kind thought of firing off smoke grenades so that I would have a sporting chance of getting away. My memory is not good on this point, but I have the impression it was the colonel himself.

Shortly after this, my own C.O. picked me up in his jeep and said he was taking me back. I said I would not go until my men were also withdrawn, and he agreed to this at once. Of the seventy-five men I had taken into the battle, only eleven were left who were not either killed or wounded.

My C.O. was Major Baker, a man whom I liked and respected very much. He was killed in action before they reached Tunis, and his second in command, 'Tug' Wilson, became C.O. in his place. Poor 'Tug' was also killed shortly after. 'Tug' had asked for me to become his second in command, but, perhaps fortunately, I was not then fit enough for the job.

Just a passing thought: the Army had a habit of giving nicknames to go with certain surnames. Some of these were fairly obvious, like 'Dusty' Miller or 'Chalky' White, but why always 'Nobby' Clark or 'Tug' Wilson? I never found the answer to this curious and universal habit.

Chapter IV

The battle of Alamein ended, as far as I was concerned, at about four in the afternoon of the 24th October. I was taken, first by jeep, then by ambulance, to a very large tent that had been set up as a kind of clearing house for the wounded. We were laid out on stretchers packed like sardines. There was hardly room for the doctors and orderlies to move between us. Someone put a dressing on my wound and fixed it with sticky tape right round my thigh. I was to regret this later.

The poor devil in the stretcher next to me had some terrible internal injury and was slowly groaning his life away. Every breath must have been agony for him. Although I had been awake for the last thirty-six hours I could not sleep. I was not in much pain myself but I felt very conscious of the pain all around me. That tent was a kind of antechamber to hell, and I still dream about it.

The next morning I was taken in an ambulance to another forward dressing station. The poor man who had been next to me was in the same ambulance, and I could imagine how every jolt, on the rough desert track, must have been for him. By the time we arrived, he was dead.

This second forward dressing station was underground, as it was still within enemy artillery range. I was greeted by a cheerful Australian orderly who said "I'm afraid this may hurt a bit". He then pulled off the adhesive tape round my thigh, and as I am a fairly hairy man, I saw what he meant.

I was then greeted by a journalist who wanted a story. I started to tell him about the battle, but found that was not the story he wanted. He wanted to know what tune the piper played during the advance. That was the 'scoop' he was after. As it happened, I was one of the few people who could tell him. I had been within a few feet of the piper who played for the twenty minutes it took to march across open desert between our lines and the enemy. He never stopped playing, although we were under fire all the way, and of course the noise was such that one could only catch a few notes now and then. The man wanted a story, so I told him the piper played 'Scotland the Brave', and I have since read that this goes down in the history of the battle of Alamein. The truth is that he could have been playing 'Three Blind Mice' for all I could really hear.

From this dressing station I was taken by ambulance again, and as I was loaded into the ambulance, the R.A.M.C. orderly took my boots, which were placed at the foot of my stretcher with the cheerful words, "You won't be needing these again!". Up until that day I had always thought it unkind of the army to call the Royal Army Medical Corps 'Rob All My Comrades'.

At about three the following morning, we at last arrived at a real hospital in the Canal Zone of Egypt. At last I was able to lie down in a real bed. I fell fast asleep immediately, only to be woken up at six-thirty by a cheerful nurse saying it was time to wash my face, which she proceeded to do in spite of my protest that I wanted to go back to sleep.

They wasted no time at this hospital, and I was taken in to surgery. The nurse had an Irish accent, and apparently when I came to after the operation I was rambling away about what I had been doing with a beautiful Irish nurse. As the nurse had a mask over her face my imagination must have been in overdrive. I am told that this is a fairly typical side-effect of pentathol.

The surgeon took out a piece of metal not much bigger than my thumbnail. It had passed almost completely through my thigh and he took it out from the other side. The nurses gave me the piece of metal as a souvenir, and I kept it for some time. Later I discovered that it came from a

German hand grenade, not from a mortar as I had thought at the time.

While I was in that hospital I had the amusing experience of catching out the army in a 'Catch 22' situation. I was ordered to shave.

"I can't shave because I haven't got a razor, give me a razor and I will shave", I replied.

"No, we can only give a razor to other ranks, officers have to buy their own".

"But I haven't any money", I objected. (This was true, because we had emptied our pockets before going into battle, and only kept a wrist watch and a fountain pen).

"OK", they said, "we will get the pay officer to give you some money", and quite soon, an officer came round from the Pay Corps to give me some money.

"Show me your identity card" he said. (This I couldn't do, because we had to leave our identity cards with our commanding officer before we went into the battle). The Pay Corps officer quite reasonably said he could not pay me without proof of identity, which I hadn't got. Game and set to me!

In the end I was given some money and had to buy a razor and shave like a good boy, but it was fun while it lasted.

The ward next to ours was for officers suffering from jaundice. At that time no-one seemed to realise that hepatitis is infectious, so the jaundice patients wandered in and out of our ward quite freely. There were twenty officers in the 'wounded' ward and six of us, including me, caught jaundice.

From this hospital in Egypt, I was taken by hospital train to Jerusalem to a very good, real, permanent hospital. While I was there we received a radio programme to say that people at home had heard of the great victory of Alamein and the church bells all over England were rung for the first time since the war had started. Tears of emotions came to my eyes when I heard English church bells ringing, England seemed such a long way away.

My wound in the leg had really done me very little damage, but I was very sick with jaundice, a most depressing illness.

I have one or two memories of hospital. One was when a nurse gave me a bath and she said with some horror, "When did you last have a bath?" I told her that I could not remember exactly but it was about five months ago.

Another memory is of the time when I was due to be discharged from the Jerusalem hospital, and the Surgeon Colonel in charge of the hospital told me that as I had suffered from jaundice I must not touch alcohol for at least twelve months. I said it was a pity he had not told me earlier, as on the previous night I had gone with a friend to the King David Hotel for dinner and had drunk a bottle of wine. I also pointed out that whilst I had been in his hospital I had been given a glass of whisky every evening. Apparently he did not know this, and it must have come as a bit of a shock. I did not tell him that I simply had not been able to drink the whisky because the smell of it made me feel sick.

From Jerusalem, I was sent to a convalescent depot somewhere in Palestine. It was like a holiday camp, and I was able to do a little riding as they had some horses. It was near the sea, but it was winter by then, and too cold to bathe, at least for me.

Eventually I was pronounced fit enough to return to 'light duties' and was sent to the Royal Engineer depot at Ismailia, on the Suez Canal, which was a sort of holding camp where everyone was sent when they first arrived from England.

The Commanding Officer of this depot was Colonel Klautman, a V.C. and M.C. from the 1914-18 war. He had been a K.C. (that is to say a senior barrister) before the war, and was to become a judge after the war was over. Klautman gave me a job as instructor at the Depot, first in mines and explosives and later in all the other aspects of Engineer work. I soon found out that the best way to learn anything is to have to teach it. I kept myself one day ahead of the class by reading up my next lesson the evening before. It was often a quite close run thing. I particularly enjoyed all forms of rope work, and this later came in handy when, after the war, I took to sailing.

Among other officers and men passing through were officers from Palestine (at that time the State of Israel did not exist), and I found them very interested in all aspects of explosives. They were my star pupils, and I probably trained some of the Israeli 'terrorists' who were such a danger to the British peace keepers after the war.

To come back to Colonel Klautman, after he had made me part of his staff I always dined at High Table with him and the other senior officers. He was a man of great wit and charm, presiding rather like a genial host over a mess that often had as many as eighty officers.

One of Klautman's bright ideas was to get hold of some horses. He found out that the Scots Greys had left their horses in Palestine when they became mechanised, and these horses were eating their heads off without anything to do. The Colonel managed to have three of these horses sent to Ismailia by rail, together with their Arab groom to look after them.

One of these remounts was a magnificent chestnut mare and the Colonel naturally picked her for himself. This mare proved to be a vicious and quite uncontrollable beast. Even the Arab groom was afraid to go into the box with her. The very first time the Colonel rode her she threw him off, and when the Adjutant had the privilege of riding her he had no better luck than the Colonel, and the beast was passed to mugsy, meaning me.

I decided that before I would attempt to ride the animal, we must become friends, and so I spent several hours talking to her in her loose box. At first she put her ears back, showed the whites of her eyes and started biting the door of her box and making it clear that she wanted to kill anyone who came near her. Eventually I managed to calm her down enough for her to allow me into her box and put my hand on her neck. After a time she had completely calmed down and even let me kiss her on the nose.

The next morning I took her out for a ride. The American Air Force had started making a landing strip in the desert - a long strip of flat sand - and I took my mare (she had the ridiculous name of Merry Legs) onto the landing strip and let her gallop the full length. It was a wonderful experience for both of us, and after that she was happy again. I think she had been cooped up without exercise for so long that she had become mad with frustration. I was allowed to keep this wonderful Merry Legs as my personal mount, and we had a lot of fun together.

Ismailia was a very pleasant place to be stationed. As well as having a horse to ride, we could go sailing on Lake Timsah. The R.E. had several of its own sailing boats, and of course we could swim in the lake and in the Canal.

Another rather naughty and unethical sport was 'fishing' for red mullet with a small piece of explosive. The explosion stunned the fish and we could pick them out of the water.

You had to be careful that your balls were not in the water when the explosion went off. I never had this experience, but I knew someone who did, and he was never quite the same afterwards.

Chapter V

It was at the R.E. Depot in Ismailia that I first met 'Dick' Turpin. At that time, I spent the evenings in the mess playing poker with another ex-desert officer. We were trying to part the newly arrived officers from the two months back pay they would receive on arrival in Egypt. We were both pretty good at it, and at one time I was winning more at poker than I was paid by the Army, not that that was very much.

Dick Turpin was a vicar's son. He was a blue eyed, fair-haired boy with a face that didn't appear to need a shave, and my friend and I thought he was a lamb for the shearing. We couldn't have been more wrong. Dick took us both to the cleaners. I was to meet Dick (his real name was James) twice more before the war was over and we became very close friends. He won the MC in Holland and lost a leg there. Years later, whenever he stayed with us at our house in Bramhall, my daughters were fascinated by the wooden leg, which he took off at night. In fact my eldest daughter sometimes used to hide it. The leg was called Horace.

While I was at the R.E. Depot, I was posted as an instructor to the School of Military Engineering which was a few miles down (or up?) the Canal from Ismailia. This gave me promotion to Captain and a fairly cushy job in a very comfortable spot. Although I had lost my horse, there was a rowing boat called a Gibralta Gig at the S.M.E. and six of us used to take it for a row along the Suez Canal nearly every day.

Looking back on it, I cannot think of a more comfortable and safe place to be at that stage of the war, and you might imagine that I was completely happy there. Nothing could be further from the truth. I had been separated from the woman I loved for two years and was quite desperately miserable about it. You might also wonder why I did not write home more often, and the answer is that all our letters were censored. That meant that you could not say where you were or what you were doing, which left little room for anything else to say except 'I love you' in one way or another, and knowing that someone else is going to read your letters rather inhibits one's style.

While I was stuck in the Canal Zone, the Eighth Army had advanced to Tunisia and was getting nearer to England, via Italy perhaps, or by boat direct to the UK ready for the invasion of France. I was told that it was no use applying for a different posting. The S.M.E. was stuck in Egypt for the rest of the war and I was stuck with it.

There was, however, a way out of this fix. They could not refuse a posting to a parachute unit, and the Royal Engineers had a parachute squadron in Tunisia.

That is why I became a parachutist.

By that time, my leg wound had completely healed and my jaundice had done me no permanent harm, I was as fit as a flea with swimming, riding and rowing.
The only snag was that I was short-sighted and could not pass the medical for that reason. Just as love is said to laugh at locksmiths, in my case it laughed at medical inspections.

The Medical Officer had two sight boards and I memorised the top letter (the only one I could read without glasses) and the bottom line of both sight boards.

That is how I became a parachutist.

I did my initial training at a parachute school in Palestine, somewhere near lake Tiberias, which is two thousand feet below sea level. Just for fun, we were taken for a flight over the lake so that we could say that we had flown a thousand feet below sea level, which most people simply don't believe.

Incidentally, to get to Palestine I literally hitched a lift from the American Air Force. I always found the American forces almost unbelievably helpful in any way they could be. In this case, I walked up to the American base in Ismailia. There were two sentries shooting craps at the gate when I approached, and to my surprise, instead of challenging me they stood to attention and presented arms, which was pretty impressive. I got to see the duty officer and told him that I had to get to Palestine and could he help.

"Yes", he said, "Sure thing. We have a plane going there this afternoon." So I was given a lift in one of their Dakotas.

I had only just started my training when I was told to go and join the parachute squadron in Tunisia. By the way, one of the conditions of my posting was that I had to agree to give up my rank of Captain, as there was no vacancy for a Captain in the unit, so now I was once again a Lieutenant. My journey to Tunisia, by train to Alexandria and by boat to Sfax, was quite uneventful.

The worst part of parachute training was the very hard physical endurance training we had to go through. After that, the jumps themselves were the easy part. We were also put through a very thorough course in the art of killing people, both with various weapons and bare-handed. I am happy to say that I was never actually called upon to exercise these skills, but if times get hard, I could probably still hire myself out as a fully qualified assassin.

My first jump was exciting. We jumped out of a Dakota aircraft, which has a side passenger door. Before you jump, a red light comes on and the dispatcher shouts "Action Stations". You all stand up in a line to go through the open door and when the green light comes on, you go.

The big surprise is that the slipstream hits you really hard and knocks you sideways. After that, the next surprise is the total silence. There you are, hanging quite still in space with only the distant sound of the disappearing aircraft. You have the impression of not moving, but when you look down you see that the earth is rocking from side to side and coming up to meet you quite slowly, then you realise that the earth is coming up rather quickly and you hit it fairly hard. You tuck your elbows into your sides and try to roll as you were taught to do in training. I must have got it right because I hadn't broken anything and was not hurt any worse than from a fall when skiing.

We had to do five jumps to qualify for the parachute badge and the red beret, and all five were much the same except for the night jump, which I found a bit unnerving, but not really any more difficult.

One heard stories of the 'Roman Cradle'. That was the name given for when the parachute failed to open. It did happen sometimes in those days, but I never saw one. One also heard stories of landing in bad spots like rocks or buildings. At that time, one could not steer the parachute like you can today, so you could not select your landing place.

One unlucky jumper landed in a prickly pear hedge and had to have spines removed from his body, some of them in rather sensitive places. Another landed on the back of a cow - and I heard of one who actually landed in a well and had to be pulled out by his harness.

Anyway, there we all were in North Africa, a fully trained Parachute Division waiting for action. And waiting, and waiting, and waiting.

We were told of a plan to drop us on Rome airport, combined with a sea landing at Anzio. This would effectively cut off the Germans in the

South and was to coincide with the surrender of the Italian army. For some reason, this plan was never put into action, and there was nothing useful for us to do, so we were sent on holiday to the Atlas Mountains, where we camped out and went climbing.

It was on one of these climbs that I had my close encounter with a baboon. I was climbing up what is called a 'chimney', which means that you have your back on one side of a gap in the rock and your feet on the other side. I was leading about four other officers, who were below me in the chimney, when I discovered that there was a troop of about twenty baboons above me. Baboons have a nasty habit of throwing stones. Fortunately, their aim is not very good and they always throw back-handed.

Luckily they did not start throwing stones, but when I got to the top of the chimney I came face to face with the leader of the troop. He was about the size of an Alsatian dog, with very dog-like teeth, and he was about three feet in front of my face going 'whoo, whoo, whoo' and bouncing up and down. I had never met a baboon socially before, so I just said 'whoo, whoo, whoo' back, and to my relief this was the correct reply, because he backed off and gave me no further trouble.

The country round the Atlas mountains was really lovely and the villages looked very French, not at all Arabic. We would have been happy to spend more time there, but one day we were told to go to Bizerte for embarkation to Italy, and so we were gathered together in bits and pieces and taken by road to Bizerte, where we embarked on a Royal Navy Cruiser and set off for Taranto.

On the way to Taranto, we saw the Italian Navy ships steaming in the opposite direction. We had been told that they were out of the war, but our Navy was taking no chances, and every navy gun was pointed at the Italian fleet. If one of the

Italian guns had turned towards us, our guns would have fired. Fortunately the Italians kept their guns pointing fore and aft and so nothing happened. I was not in the least afraid of the Italians firing at us, but I was really scared that our cruiser might start shooting. As we were all on the cruiser's deck we would have lost our eardrums!

Our fleet sailed into Taranto harbour completely unopposed. The Germans didn't even know we were there and not a shot was fired. By very bad luck one of our cruisers was blown up and sunk in the harbour by a magnetic mine, I saw the ship go down stern first and could hear the cries of the men on board. Fortunately most of them were picked up and saved. Not so fortunately, all the Parachute Division artillery was on that boat and was lost. It was very stupid to have put what little artillery we had all on the same ship. I don't know who was responsible for that.

Someone had made arrangements for an Italian Horse Artillery troop to join us, and to everyone's surprise they duly turned up. They were a cheerful bunch and very proud of their guns, which they galloped about rather like the Royal Horse Artillery doing their performance at Earls Court. I don't think they ever had occasion to fire their guns, and I don't think there was ever a target for them to shoot at, as I will explain later.

The first engineering job we were called upon to do was to blow up a fairly large stone bridge over a river near Taranto.

Now steel bridges are quite easy to blow up, and steel suspension bridges are even easier: you just have to cut the elastic and their knickers fall down, so to speak. But stone bridges need a lot of explosives, which we did not have. Being parachutists, we had no transport and everything we had was carried on our backs.

Someone found a German minefield near the bridge, so we dug up the mines and took out the explosives. It took us a whole day to do this job, and while we were doing it a German truck drove up with some lucky soldiers on board who were driving into Taranto for a night out on the town. They were very surprised to find out that the British had landed.

When we had finished preparing the bridge for demolition and were waiting for the order to blow it up, a message came from Monty, who had just been put in charge of operations, to say that he needed the bridge to be left intact as he wanted to bring his troops across it, so we spent the next day un-preparing the bridge for demolition. This bridge nonsense was to have quite serious long-term effects that we knew nothing about at the time.

While we had been in North Africa we had taken anti-malaria tablets every day, even though there is very little malaria in North Africa. But what the medical services didn't know was that malaria was very common in that part of Italy at that time, and no precautions were taken. We were plagued by mosquitoes while we were working on the bridge, and many of us, myself included, caught malaria, which is a long term problem - and in many cases revisited us during the Normandy campaign. I have suffered from bouts of malaria ever since.

The reason for sending us to Taranto was that it was hoped that the Germans would divert some of their troops from the Allied landings on the west coast, where things were getting rather sticky. If that really was the plan it didn't work. The Germans took no notice of us whatsoever.

It was a bit insulting in a way. First of all a parachute unit having to go in by boat - and then an enemy who didn't bother to fight! By an odd coincidence, the only German forces in the south-east of Italy were the German First

Parachute Division, so there was the makings of a first class ding-dong battle between so-called elite troops. It didn't happen. The German First Parachute Division had been ordered to draw back and hold a line somewhere further north. The result was that we marched into village after village, only to learn that the Germans had marched out the day before. We never met!

As I have said, we had no transport and had to carry everything on our backs. However, some clever chap got hold of a dozen or so pack mules that had been used by the Italian army. My men were nearly all city bred and had no experience of horses or mules, so the men and the mules took an immediate dislike to one another. The strange thing is that after only a few days they became the best of friends, and it was not uncommon on a cold night, when we were sleeping out in the open, to find men snuggled up against the mules for warmth.

At one time, we were billeted in a farm at a village called Gioia del Colle. I had been allocated a splendid riding mule who would put up a terrific fight against being saddled and bridled, but once that was done he was as gentle as a lamb, and I spent many happy hours riding him.

We had a man in our troop who had one of the ugliest faces I have ever seen, except perhaps on the gargoyles of Notre Dame in Paris. He was a Glaswegian with an almost unintelligible accent, but apart from all that he was a very good and useful man to have in the troop. One day this man bet me a bar of chocolate that he could saddle and bridle my mule single handed. It seemed like an easy bet, so I accepted. To my surprise, he did the trick with no trouble at all. He had discovered that the mule would do anything for a handful of sugared almonds. I later discovered why he wanted the chocolate: the farmer's daughter would do anything for a bar of chocolate.

I have one more mule story, which illustrates just how tough these splendid animals can be. One day a farmer came to us in great distress, to say that his mule had fallen down a well. Could we help? As we really had nothing useful to do, we were glad of the chance to do something. What had happened was that the mule was pulling a plough when the ground collapsed under him and he fell into an underground aqueduct, probably built hundreds of years ago by the Romans.

The first job was to lower a man down the hole to fasten a rope to the plough and pull it out of the way. While this was being done, I managed to use some of the skills I had learned at the School of Military Engineering and rigged up a simple crane using some telegraph poles that we found and some rope and blocks that were part of our equipment. We managed to put two rope slings under the belly of the mule and started to haul him up. This upset the poor beast so much that in his struggles he got the ropes round his neck so that we had to lower him pretty quickly, before he choked to death.

At this point, I felt that I would lose face with my men if we failed to rescue the mule, so rather reluctantly I stripped off and was lowered down myself. I can still remember that the water was bloody cold. I fixed a rope round each of his four legs - it would be very uncomfortable for the mule but he would not be able to kick them off. I then gave the order to haul us both up together. The mule was pretty quiet by now and gave no trouble, so that he was hauled up quite easily. It must have been a rather unusual sight for the natives of Gioia del Colle, who by this time had turned up en masse to see what was going on. There was I, sitting stark naked on the back of a very wet mule hanging in the air from a rope. In the words of one of my favourite quotes from Josephine Baker, "I wasn't really naked, I simply didn't have any clothes on".

The next morning the mule was back at work ploughing the field.

My memory of the Italian campaign is of marching mile after mile over very hilly country, fortunately by now with mules to carry most of our equipment, and of sleeping on the ground in the open night after night. We did not carry either tents or camp beds, and the ground was often stony and always very cold. One morning I woke up to find that my trousers were frozen to the ground, and I had a terrible pain in my right hip. That day we marched another twenty miles or more, and every step was agony. Fortunately that night someone produced some very good Chianti, and I got myself seriously drunk, which completely cured the pain. I wonder now if that night was the cause of the arthritis that I got fifty years later? It certainly confirmed my belief in the therapeutic value of red wine.

The poor mules all caught a cold, they were coughing and wheezing and disgusting snot was hanging out of their noses. Unfortunately we did not have a vet with us, but there was probably not much a vet could have done. As with humans, there is really no cure for a cold and it simply had to take its course. About four or five days of misery.

My daughter Angie remarked when she started reading these memoirs that I was always writing about food. This is true, I am afraid. Food, or the lack of it, was very much in people's mind during the war years, and those of us who lived through it still find it difficult to waste food, so here is another little comment on the subject.

When we were at Gioia del Colle, I noticed that the field behind the farm was covered with mushrooms, so I started gathering them. The farmer's wife and his family became very agitated and told us they were poisonous. They watched in horror when we sat down to eat a feast of them, and kept crossing themselves and muttering and shaking their heads slowly. The next morning when they found to their surprise that we were all alive and well, they rushed out into the field and started gathering mushrooms for themselves. I have no doubt that they would eat all kinds of fungus that the English would call toadstools, but for some reason had not found out that what **we** call mushrooms are edible.

Before I leave the Italian part of my story I would like to tell you of a little adventure that happened to a friend of mine called Peter (I can't remember his surname) who was sent on a special mission to occupy the radio station in Bari with a small party of four or five men. At that time we hadn't 'taken' Bari, but the Germans were very thin on the ground and he didn't have any trouble. The job he had to do was to hold the radio station for some Italian big-wig (I think it was Count Sforza), to broadcast to the Italian people that Italy was no longer fighting the British and American troops. The broadcast was made, and Peter decided to spend that night in the best hotel in Bari, the Hotel Imperiale, where he requisitioned the bridal suite. Peter was a tall, fair-haired very English looking officer, with the good looks that Italian ladies often fall for. Peter had the good fortune to be introduced to a charming Italian lady in the bar of the Hotel and evidently she liked the idea of sharing the Bridal Suite with him.

Apparently everything went according to plan until the next morning, when the manager came up to his room in great agitation to say that the Germans had arrived. Peter strolled onto the balcony in front of his room and saw two German armoured cars in front of the hotel, so he ordered the manager to send up breakfast for two and went back to bed. Well, the Italians had been told to offer their services to the British, and Peter liked his home comforts.

Rescuing a mule from a well and introducing the natives to mushrooms are the only two useful things I did during my Italian campaign, apart, perhaps, from making one Glaswegian and one chocoholic Italian girl very happy.

I never saw a German soldier, apart from the little party that drove into us on the way to a night out in Taranto. I never fired a shot or heard a shot fired, we didn't blow anything up, or build any bridges, or clear any minefields, so I don't know whether to call this chapter 'Much Ado About Nothing', or perhaps 'A Comedy of Errors'.

However, my original objective in becoming a parachutist was achieved, because in December the whole parachute division was shipped back to England.

Chapter VI

Like nearly everything I had experienced with the Parachute Brigade, the journey home did not go according to plan.

Our ship developed engine trouble, and we were taken off at Algiers. We were billeted in sleeping cars which had been left in a siding (quite comfortable and luxurious after what we had been used to in Italy). We were to be taken from Algiers in two ships which had been directed to two quays in the harbour. For some reason I had been given the job of baggage officer. I had to store the Parachute Division's baggage on the two quays allocated to the two ships that were to take us all back to England, home and glory.

For some reason that I have never been able to understand, I had a very clear vision of the two ships coming into the harbour and going to the wrong two quays. I was so certain of this that I made a thorough nuisance of myself going to everyone I could think of, from the divisional headquarters to the Algiers harbour master, telling them that I thought there had been a mistake. I was told, very properly, to get on with the job and not ask silly questions. As you can imagine, there was a lot of baggage, and it took us two days to load it all onto the quays. Incidentally, it is odd that there was so much baggage going out, when we came in with only what we could carry on our backs, but that was how it was.

The day came, and I stood on the quay as the two ships steamed into the harbour and went directly to the wrong berths, exactly as I had 'seen' it. I have never had premonitions before or since this time, but when I had this one I had no doubt whatsoever. I was absolutely certain what would happen. It took us a whole day and a half to rearrange the baggage to the right quays, and certainly no-one thanked me for being such a nuisance.

We eventually boarded our ship on Christmas Day. It was pouring with rain as we stood on the quay, we had no Christmas dinner, (in fact we had no dinner at all), but you have never seen such a happy group of people. We were going home.

The voyage from Algiers to England was uneventful. Unfortunately the American services were in control of everything, so it was a 'dry' ship. However, I had taken the precaution of smuggling a bottle of Scotch aboard, so I survived the voyage with no great hardship.

The Army likes to give officers duties to carry out, whether or not they are really useful. It is the principle of the thing! On this occasion they came up with a real beauty. We officers were sent up to a look-out point, in rotation, to report in case we were attacked from the air or from the sea.

It was very cold up there, but otherwise quite pleasant to watch the sea and the sky, something that I have always enjoyed. There were three telephones in the look-out, and so I thought it would be a good idea to check them out.

I got no answer at all from the first two telephones, but on the third attempt, after some five or ten minutes, I got an answer. I asked who I was talking to, and was told not to ask silly questions, what had it got to do with me who I was talking to? I explained that I was in the look-out post. "Never heard of it", I was told. I said I was there to spot air raids or other forms of attack. "Oh yes, and what would I do about it if we were attacked?" I said all I could do was telephone someone and tell them about it.

I was told in no uncertain manner that no-one would take any notice of anyone except their own ship's officers. I could see his point of view - and had to admire the command of the English language that he showed in telling me, more or less, where I could put the telephone. It was a cold night and a long one, but I was happy.

We landed in Liverpool and I found a telephone kiosk on the quayside, so I dialled Pinner 26 and to my surprise got through straight away. I hadn't heard June's voice for nearly three years and can't begin to describe how I felt, and then a voice that I had never heard before said "Hello Daddy!"

It took a few days before I had leave, but we eventually met in the Savoy Hotel. I found that they had given us a room with twin beds, so naturally I had to change the room.

While I had been on a walking tour of southern Italy, June had been in far greater danger from the air raids over London and sometimes over Pinner. She also had to endure the VI 'flying bomb', which came over southern England night and day, every night and every day. June remembers pushing Franky in the pram, when a V1 stopped overhead. She didn't know which way to run, so she just carried on walking, whistling a happy tune – and obviously lived to tell the tale.

On another occasion, she was in the greengrocer's when the shopkeeper referred to her as "Mrs Junker" (at the time, Junkers were feared enemy planes). June, who is the eldest daughter of a proud air-force family (her father was a WW1 flying hero and in WW2 he was the founder of 604 squadron) was outraged. "My name is 'Jucker', not Junker", she said. "It's a Swiss name, and my husband it out there somewhere, fighting the Germans to protect England." The poor greengrocer never made that mistake again – and to be fair, the names do sound very similar.

June thought that if she described the bombers as 'puffer trains', this might seem less frightening to Franky. But she remembers one night in Pinner when she heard a flying bomb coming over, and Franky said,

"That's a train, isn't it, Mummy?"

"Yes darling", said June, "it's a train".

"There'll be a big bang soon, won't there Mummy?"

I suppose it's quite surprising that my eldest daughter didn't grow up with a morbid fear of trains.

We did not have very long together before I got my next posting. The War Office had decided that they had far too many parachute officers in proportion to the number of parachute trained other ranks, so it was a case of last in first out, and I was out. I was very upset at the time, but have come to realise that it was part of the good luck that had been with me right through the war, because the First Parachute Division were later to be dropped on Arnhem, and not many came back.

I was, however, very pleased to be posted to the 4th Field Squadron, which was the most famous squadron in the Eighth Army in North Africa and part of the 7th Armoured Division. So I now wore the Desert Rat symbol on my arm, of which I was as proud as I had been to wear the red beret of the Airborne Division.

We spent some time training in Ripon on the construction of the Bailey Bridge, which I might describe as grown-up Meccano. This was equipment that we had never seen in Africa or in Italy, so the training was very necessary for all of us.

We old veterans of the Desert War were very surprised at the attitude of the army that had stayed in England. They were all so ruddy keen and Spartan. In the Eighth Army, we had learned that any damn fool can make himself uncomfortable, and the obvious way to survive was to avail oneself of every comfort that came to hand. The home troops, on the other hand, seemed to regard any comfort available as being too soft and unsoldierly. This was **very** different from the style of the 7th Armoured Division!

Eventually, of course, the day was approaching for us to go to France. We were very upset to learn that we would not be landed on D Day, but the day after.

Monty in his usual way had to talk in terms of cricket and in an attempt to make us feel less left out, he told us that "One does not put one's best batsman in to bat first." In hindsight, it was an outrageous comparison, but proved to be just as well for me, and part of my usual luck to miss the worst of that great blood-bath.

I remember looking at the green corn springing up all over England and wondering whether I would live to see it harvested. We all knew what was involved on the shores of France, and I don't think many of us would have given it better than an even chance.

Chapter VII

In *Henry V,* Shakespeare says, "Fair set the wind for France", but on this occasion there was rather more wind than we wanted. We went across from Tilbury on an American Liberty ship, until the coast of France was about one mile off. My troop was then transferred to a tank landing craft.

The captain of the landing craft was an American, and he called out to me,

"Lootenant, will you please come up here". I went up to the little bridge and he asked me where we wanted to be landed, and I told him

"Gold Beach".

"Oh", he said, "I don't know where that would be". This was a bit of a setback, because the arrangement was that the Navy was responsible for getting us to the right place. Anyway, he said,

"I know a nice spot where you won't even get your feet wet." In fact he was right, and we didn't get our feet wet, but it took us an hour or two to find our way to the place where we were supposed to be.

There was nothing very dramatic going on along the coast, the heavy fighting had all been done the day before. There was still some shell-fire and the occasional German fighter plane shooting up the landing area, but nothing really heavy.

I am not going to give you an account of the advance through Normandy. You can read it up in the historical records, and in any case my memory is now confused as to which event came before or after another. I will just give you a general impression and fill in a few details in which I was personally involved.

It was the job of the 4th Field Squadron to clear obstacles (mines) and build bridges where required, to make it possible for the 7th Armoured Division to move over the ground. In the early days of the campaign, our tanks did not have any serious opposition from German tanks. Fortunately, Hitler had held back his Panzer division to defend Calais, because he believed that the Normandy landings were a diversion. Eventually, of course, he realised his mistake and moved his Panzers into Normandy.

At this point, I would like to make a few remarks on the general principles of tank fighting. To simplify the business, the intention was that our tanks should have a gun that would make a hole in the enemy tanks, and that our tanks had armour that the enemy guns could not penetrate. Naturally the Germans had the same idea, but, unfortunately for us, they did it better!

The 7th Armoured Division met the German Tiger tanks at Villers-Bocage, and it was a massacre. The German guns went right through our tanks, and our tank guns could not get through the German armour. We had to 'withdraw', which is the technical word for running away. It was muggins' job (me and my troop being muggins) to be the last to leave and to mine the road as we went.

I had already experienced this rather spooky task at Alam Halfa in North Africa and had the same feelings again. Everything is suddenly so quiet. Our own troops have gone and the enemy does not yet realise this.

We were lucky. The German tanks did not come that night, and we managed to get to Tilly-sur-Seule without any trouble, having laid mines in the road behind us. At Tilly we had another battle, but somehow managed to fight some sort of rearguard action.

There is a dead straight road north of Tilly with poplars in a line on each side of it. These trees had all been cut off at the base by gunfire. The fields all round us were full of dead cows and occasional horses, their bodies blown up like barrage balloons and their four legs sticking up in the air. There was the slightly sweet, nauseating smell of death everywhere, and it wasn't only from dead animals.

It was in a farm somewhere near Tilly where I saw my men really frightened: the only time a group of them ran past me in a mad panic. I thought the entire German Panzer Korps must be behind them. Then I saw what the panic was about and ran too. They had knocked over a beehive, and the whole swarm was chasing them.

Somehow, the tide of battle changed in our favour, and we started advancing again. The next big battle was for Caen. I remember the Division of tanks advancing and the anti-tank guns of the Germans firing at us, and hoped that the German gunners would not waste a shot on my armoured car, but would concentrate on the tanks.

We took Caen, what was left of it. It was nearly all reduced to rubble. I managed to find a ground floor room for us, for the night, which kept off the rain, and in the morning I discovered it must have been part of the Bishop's Palace. In a cupboard, there was a magnificent silver chalice. We left this where we found it, but I don't know if the bishop ever got it back.

My next fairly clear memory is of a town called St. Pierre-sur-Dives. This was the only town, apart from Bayeux, that was almost left standing. We had a rather sick joke about this, and said it evidently had not been liberated.

A very kind French family invited me to spend the night in their house, and I was delighted to accept. For weeks we had all been sleeping in slit trenches because the Luftwaffe knew exactly where to find us and bombed us every night. It poured with rain night after night, and I looked forward to having a roof over my head for a change. The French family, father, mother and rather good-looking daughter, wanted to spend the night in their air-raid shelter in the garden. That night I went to bed in clean sheets. I took with me my revolver and an electric torch, just in case (in case of what I am not sure, but not all the French were as pro-Allies as one might expect, or so we had been warned).

The German bombers came and bombed the town from end to end. The plaster fell from my bedroom ceiling and the windows rattled but did not break. Then it was quiet. Not a sound except for the creak of my bedroom door. I sat up in bed with my revolver in one hand and my torch in the other. I felt a light pressure on my foot, and then a light pressure creeping up my leg. Was it the daughter or the assassin? I did not raise my hopes too much, but it was an interesting situation. I switched on my torch and looked straight into the eyes of a very small and very frightened kitten.

This story has a very sad ending. The German bombs that had missed the house made a direct hit on the air raid shelter, and all the family were killed.

I am sometimes asked, "Weren't you ever frightened?" and of course I was, many times. But I still remember one occasion when I was more frightened than ever. I had been sent on a night patrol to have a look at a deep ditch or cutting to see if it would be an obstacle to our tanks. The snag was that the Germans were occupying this ditch at the time. There was an open field in front of the ditch, and hedges running across the field on either side. Although the hedges would have given me some cover, it seemed likely that the enemy would be particularly careful to watch there, so I decided to creep across in the middle of the field.

It was a pitch dark night, and I thought I might just get away with it. Suddenly something alerted the Germans and they fired up several Very lights, which lit up like full daylight, and at the same time they opened up with two or more machine guns. The grass was only a few inches high, and I felt sure the enemy could see me. They raked the field from side to side for what seemed like hours, but was probably only about twenty minutes. The field was quite flat, there was nowhere to hide, and I expected to feel my body raked by machine gun fire.

I remember a rather silly thought passing through my mind. I said to myself that I would willingly pay two thousand pounds to be in Scott's Bar in Piccadilly instead of in that field in Normandy. It was a silly thought because, apart from anything else, I would not have been able to raise two thousand pounds. Somehow or other I survived and always remembered that moment every time I went to Scott's Bar after the war. Like so many great watering holes in London, today Scott's Bar no longer exists.

After this completely unsuccessful venture, I was told to take a look at the 'ditch' from the air, and accordingly I was taken up in a Lysander, which is a small aeroplane used for artillery spotting. It was the same plane as was flown by Brian Gibb in Italy. (Brian was a great friend of the family and was the Godfather of my eldest daughter. He was one of the very few Army Officers to be awarded the D.F.C).

Unfortunately my pilot got lost and decided to come down low to have a look at where we were. One Normandy village looks very like another from the air: the same stone Norman church and the same square, with people walking around in it. The 'people', I noticed, were wearing grey uniforms and shooting at us, so we made a rather sharp exit. I never did get to see that ditch, and it really didn't make any difference, because the next attack didn't go in that direction.

I can't say that we liked the Germans, but we were always impressed by their technical skills, particularly in camouflage. I can remember overhearing a conversation over our radio which went rather like this: "Do you see the haystacks in the field in front of us? The third one from the left just moved." They had disguised their anti-tank guns to look like Normandy haystacks.

About that time, I had a personal experience of their ability at camouflage and also of their discipline. The 22nd Armoured Brigade, to which our Squadron was attached, was commanded by a delightful chap called Brigadier Hinds. He was affectionately known as 'Loony Hinds' because, unlike the Duke of Plazatoro (who led his regiment from behind), Loony Hinds led very much from the front. For some reason I had been sent to see the Brigadier, and was told I would find him "somewhere along the road", so off I went in my small armoured car until I came to a village called Ifs (it means yew trees in French). There was no-one there. The village appeared to be completely deserted except for a few chickens wandering about in the square. Naturally I and my driver tried without any success to catch one for dinner.

After that we went back the way we had come, and came across the Brigadier who was briefing his officers for an attack on, yes, you have guessed it, Ifs. I very wisely kept my mouth shut about our little visit to Ifs, and later that day the armoured brigade met with very heavy anti-tank fire from Ifs. I sometimes wonder what thoughts must have been in the minds of the German anti-tank gunners as they watched two silly 'Englanders' chasing chickens. They obviously thought that we were not an important enough target to be worth giving away their position by shooting us.

My next memory is about Livarot, famous for its excellent cheese. There was no fighting in

Livarot, and in a way I can claim to have 'liberated' it, as my armoured car was the first vehicle to pass through it.

Near Livarot, there was a small stream spanned by a bridge that had been blown up by the enemy. It was to be the job of my troop to build a Bailey bridge over the stream. While we were waiting for the equipment to arrive, I noticed that there was a driveway leading to a large farmhouse and then beyond it, crossing over the stream, by way of another small bridge. I reckoned this bridge was strong enough to take up to five tons, so I made a diversion for vehicles up to five tons to go round that way. The equipment arrived, and we built our little Bailey bridge over the stream, and when we had finished, the farmer invited me and my number two, 'Dick' Turpin, to have lunch with him. There was the farmer, his wife, two daughters and a son – and the Curé who, if I understood correctly, had come from Dinard. The farmer very proudly opened some bottles of Burgundy that he had buried in his garden so that the Germans would not find it: he had promised himself that he would open it up on the day he was liberated.

I did not know then that I was to meet him twice more.

The next day, I was sent for by the new General commanding the 7th Armoured Division, I am afraid I cannot remember his name, but have an impression that his appointment was a very unpopular one with the 7th Armoured. He had been appointed by Monty because the previous General had pointed out that the German anti-tank guns made holes in his tanks.

The General ordered me to go and look at a bridge that had been blown up and to let him know whether the gap could be spanned by a Turtle, which was a very ingenious bridge folded up on the top of a tank.

Off I went in a Jeep along a lane through woods and fields. I stopped briefly at a gap in the hedge, from where I could see the top of the big church at Lisieux, a town still occupied by the Germans. It was at that moment that a young girl of about eight or nine years old came up to me and gave me a red rose. At that time I did not know about St. Teresa of Lisieux or of her strange connection with red roses and I might now think that the little episode was all in my imagination. But I still had the rose in my button-hole when I was shot, and the rose was certainly real.

When I came to a bend in the lane there was a fairly large red brick building, and by it there was a small group of soldiers and one tank. I was told that the bridge I had come to see was about a hundred yards round the corner of the building and that the road was covered by a German machine gun.

One cannot disobey an order from a General, so I said that I had to go and take a look at the bridge. I also said that it would be nice and helpful if the tank came with me, in the hope that perhaps the German machine gunner would be frightened of the tank.

So I proceeded along the road, followed by the tank and nothing happened until I reached the bridge. I could see that half the bridge, the left side, had been blown, and that for some reason the explosive charges on the right side of the bridge had not been blown. There was some wire running to the explosives, but for some reason the explosives had not been fired, so I simply pulled out the detonator. At that moment the German machine gunner opened fire, and I felt a great deal of pain in my right arm. I ran like hell.

The pain in my arm was so bad that I did not know that I had also been shot through the chest. I only found out about that when I felt a wet patch on my back and discovered it was blood. Somehow I was taken up by jeep to the forward dressing station, which happened to be in the same farmhouse, and my wounds were dressed by the farmer's daughter. The farmer asked me if I would like a glass of Champagne, and I thanked him and said I would rather have some of that excellent Burgundy that he had given me the day before.

This answer must have impressed him, because, forty years later, June and I visited the area to find out whether the farmhouse was still there. It was, and when we knocked on the door, the same farmer, looking a little older, opened the door.

When I asked him if he recognised me he said, "Oh yes. You were the officer who preferred Burgundy to Champagne".

Chapter VIII

You may think it odd that I believe myself to have been lucky during the war. To give an example of my luck, I will describe something so improbable that I would not have dared to make it up.

In those days, I was rather more short-sighted than I am now, and one day I broke my glasses. It would have been possible to get an army pair to replace them, but this would have taken a few days, or possibly weeks. In the meantime I was what one calls nowadays 'visually challenged'.

The morning after breaking my glasses I was squatting in a field doing what a man has to do, when I saw, just a few feet in front of me, a pair of glasses. I tried them on and they were exactly right for my eyes. So good that I wore them for several years afterwards. There was no path through the field, and no building near the spot where I saw the glasses. If the owner had dropped them, he would have picked them up. If he had been killed there would have been a body. I have no explanation as to how the glasses came to be in that place at that time. The odds against such a thing happening must be at least as high as the odds against winning the National Lottery.

To come back to my account, after the 'dressing station' at the farmhouse I was taken to a large tented hospital, rather like those shown in the TV series *M.A.S.H.*, and there I was operated on. As usual, I was given the bullet as a souvenir. It was a 9 mm copper lead-filled bullet of the kind fired by the German Schmeitser machine gun. One bullet had apparently travelled up my right arm, smashing the radius and ulna in fifteen places. In the X-ray it looked rather like Harry Lauder's walking stick after it was patched together – and I am eternally grateful to the talented surgeon who managed to patch me up so thoroughly. Another bullet had gone clear through my chest under the clavicle and out under the right scapula – and a third had lodged somewhere near the clavicle. It was never removed, and is still with me today. Neither of these last two bullets had done me much harm, except that I could not raise my right arm above shoulder level.

After Normandy, I was flown back to a hospital in Cardiff. Fortunately this hospital had just received the first issue of penicillin and that was what really saved my arm. After a few weeks of using my bum like a pincushion, I was discharged from hospital and as far as action was concerned, my war was over.

I had very little long-term damage, apart from my right bicep, which had been detached at the bottom so that I had virtually no muscle to raise my right arm. I set myself a rigorous course of training by trying to raise half a pint of bitter to my mouth with my right arm. After six months, I was able to raise a full pint and I was more or less cured.

Evidently I was reasonably fit by then, because nine months later, my second daughter, Carolyn, was born. It was during June's pregnancy that I was called to Buckingham Palace to receive my M.C. On the big day, June was suffering from severe morning sickness, and was very nearly sick on the Royal Carpet!

The injury to my right shoulder was more or less cured twenty-two years later by a lucky accident on the yacht Zen, when I fell backwards onto the saloon table. This broke the lesion (I am not sure if this is the correct term), and after a time I had complete freedom of movement of my right arm, except perhaps that I can't turn my wrist to take coins in my right hand and still have pain in my shoulder after fifty odd years.

Looking back on things, one tends to talk about the enemy as the Germans, but for the first two years in North Africa the enemy were the Italians, and even at the battle of El Alamein the division on **my** bit of the front was the Italian Trento division, so I was wounded and my men were killed by Italians and not by Germans.

People sometimes write off the Italian army as useless, but the fact is that a gun fired by an Italian does just as much damage to bone and tissue as a gun fired by a German.

Italians will probably tell you that they never supported Mussolini, but really what they don't like about Il Duce is that he didn't win. If the Italians and Germans had won the war you would find that nearly all the Italians would claim to have been members of the Fascist Party. I feel I should be allowed to say a few slightly detrimental things about the Italians, as I have Italian blood in my veins (my grandfather was Swiss Italian). In any case, I am sure that my Italian/Jewish brother in law, Elio, would have agreed wholeheartedly with this observation.

It is fashionable today to have 'counselling' after any fairly traumatic experience, and I am very glad my generation was spared this experience after the war. We managed to work out our own adjustments to life.

Perhaps one of the after-effects of the war for us is that the problems of life all seem rather trivial and unimportant and that the love and health of one's family are the only things that really matter.

After I was discharged from hospital, I was posted to an Officer Training Unit in Newark as an instructor. As I was an expert in mines and explosives I was naturally given the job of instructor in mathematics, and as before, in Ismailia, I found myself trying hard to be one lesson ahead of my class.

The O.C.T.U. as it was called, at Newark, had about forty or fifty officers in the Officers' Mess, and I was given the job of mess secretary. By a bit of luck I had a very well qualified mess sergeant who had been the head waiter at Oddenino's Restaurant in London, so we were able to dish up some reasonably edible grub in the mess.

They gave me back the rank of Captain that I had given up in North Africa in order to become a parachutist.

Looking back on it, I seem to have done things for the wrong reasons. I became an Engineer so that I could go skiing, and a parachutist so that I could get back to England.

Let me finish with a quote from *Henry V*:

'Old men forget; yet all shall be forgot,
But he'll remember, with advantages,
What feats he did that day.'

[Act IV, scene iii]

If I have added some 'advantages' in my story it is not intentional, but certainly this old man forgot many things, so that events and names and places are often confused in my memory.

To the question "What did you do in the war, Daddy?" I can only say "We won".

But in the words of Wellington after Waterloo, "It was a damned close run thing".

Printed in Great Britain
by Amazon